Anonymous

Honduras and the Perry Land Grant

A new field for the farmer, stockman, lumberman and laborer

Anonymous

Honduras and the Perry Land Grant
A new field for the farmer, stockman, lumberman and laborer

ISBN/EAN: 9783337311919

Printed in Europe, USA, Canada, Australia, Japan

Cover: Foto ©Lupo / pixelio.de

More available books at **www.hansebooks.com**

HONDURAS

AND

THE PERRY LAND GRANT:

A NEW FIELD

FOR THE

FARMER, STOCKMAN, LUMBERMAN

AND LABORER.

CHICAGO:

THE AMERICAN-HONDURAS CO.

1888.

PRINTED AND BOUND BY
DONOHUE & HENNEBERRY,
CHICAGO.

INDEX.

INTRODUCTORY.

Thousands of temperate, frugal, law-abiding people, skilled in the arts needed for the development of a country, have found, after years of exhausting toil and exposure to the sudden and extreme changes of an inclement climate, that they can at the best get but a bare subsistence in the North. Farmers see the interest of the mortgages on their farms increasing rapidly, to in time drive them from their homes despite their most earnest efforts. Those who have courage to calmly consider their situation see that their future offers little or no hope. Competition from the virgin fields of the West is too keen. Steam has made the farmer of the deep, rich land of Dakota and Kansas close neighbor of the man who grinds his life away on the barren soil of the East. Each short summer spent in the attempt to raise enough to support the family through the long, stormy, and cold winter only adds to the burden the hopeless strugg'e has brought.

To such people, tired of pinching along year after year in dreary although respectable poverty, these pages will be of interest, for they offer sure, safe, and speedy relief. They will be of value to young men who have wisdom to carefully look ahead, intelligence to see that life in the old and crowded fields affords little encouragement to legitimate effort, and courage and enterprise to seek new fields where competition is not sharp, and whe-e by a little toil and forethought they can quickly secure all the comforts and most of the luxuries of civilized life. To all such homes are offered in a country with'n easy reach, where the climate is more temperate and pleasanter than in the most favored spot in the United States, and where there is freedom from many if not from all of the diseases most dangerous to human comfort and life. There the days are not hot, dry, and dusty, and the nights cold; the summers are not blistering in their droughts and the winters terrible in their blizzards; but the temperature ranges from sixty to ninety degrees .F throughout the entire year. Nearly everything that can be grown in the United States can be more easily and cheaply raised there, and many valuable crops can be produced there which can not be profitably cultivated where frosts are known.

Most of the testimony given in the following pages has been gathered from witnesses who could have had no object in favoring, since they certainly could have had no knowledge of our purposes. Much of this evidence was given thirty years ago. Several of the witnesses were

INTRODUCTORY.

officials whose standing was sufficient guaranty that their statements were trustworthy, and all of the witnesses were of a character above suspicion. Most of assertions made by them and reproduced here have been verified by recent examinations, and there is no apparent reason for doubting the entire truthfulness of any of them.

The American Honduras Company is desirous of inducing people of the character described to settle on and develope the lands granted to it, or on those belonging to the government. To this end it is prepared to sell lands to individuals or to colonists in numbers. To the latter especial inducements will be offered.

Questions addressed to the Company will receive prompt answers.

THE AMERICAN-HONDURAS CO.,

CHICAGO, ILLS., U. S. A.

THE PERRY GRANT.

For the purpose of encouraging immigration, and through that bringing about the development of the great natural resources of Honduras, the government of that republic has sold to the AMERICAN HONDURAS COMPANY a grant of land consisting of each alternate tract or section of land one myriamete῾ cr 6$\frac{6189}{10000}$ English miles square, within the following boundaries, viz.: Beginning at a point in the middle of the deepest part of the channel connecting Caratasca lagoon with the Caribbean sea, and extending thence in a northwesterly and a westerly direction along the coast of said sea to the eighty-fifth (85°) degree of longitude west from Greenwich ; thence southward along the line of said eighty-fifth (85°) degree to the place of its intersection or crossing of the fifteenth (15°) degree of latitude north from the equator ; thence eastward along the line of said fifteenth (15°) degree of latitude to the middle of the channel or bed of the river Guaranta ; thence along the middle of the channel of said river and of any lagoon or lagoons, bay or estuaries to the place where the waters of said river Guaranta join those of Caratasca lagoon ; and thence along the middle of the deepest channel in said Cara tasca lagoon to the place of beginning.

The northwestern corner of this grant is 1,800 miles south of Chicago, in longitude 8 west from Washington, and about 975 miles south by east from New Orleans. The Gulf stream touches the grant and thence flows westward and northward, hurrying vessels on their way from Central America to the markets of our Atlantic seaboard and of Europe. Vessels can have the help of this ocean current most of the way from Honduras to Europe, and back again through peaceful seas. Steamers make the run to New Orleans or to Mobile in three to four days, and to New York in seven or eight days.

The grant extends from the Caribbean sea southward nearly

5

seventy miles, and from the 84th to the 85th degree of longitude west from Greenwich. As a whole it forms a plain sloping gently from the tide water up to the low hills of the Guampu river, near the southern line of the grant. Along the coast the land is sandy loam, unsurpassed for cocoanut growing. South of the beach, at distances ranging from one to ten miles are deep, clear sounds or lagoons of salt water, much like those lying south of Cape Hatteras. Some of these lagoons are connected with each other by navigable channels, and all of them may be so connected by digging a few miles of canal through low and soft ground. Around the lagoons are large areas of rich alluvium where bananas, plantains, sugarcane, breadfruit, sweet potatoes, yampas, yams, cassava, rice, and many other crops grow luxuriantly. Beyond this alluvial belt are prairies which afford abundant pasturage on which stock remain fat throughout the entire year. Groves of long leaved pine are scattered over these prairies. Along the streams and on the hills valuable cabinet woods abound, and medicinal plants are dispersed through every forest. The natural productions of this region are many and of great value, finding ready market in the United States and Europe, as well as in the towns scattered along the shores of the Carribean sea.

Cocoanut and other palms thrive all along the sea and around the lagoons. Each cocoanut tree bears from sixty to three hundred nuts per year, the crop from an acre being worth from $60 to $300. Bananas and plantains yield as large, sure, and uniform returns, the income therefrom averaging from $75 to $300 an acre per annum. Pineapples give profits fully equal to those mentioned above, while vanilla, cacao, limes, lemons, oranges, and a long list of other fruits may easily be made to give profitable employment to thousands of people, and afford very large gains.

Mahogany and other valuable woods can be put aboard vessels in the harbors on the northern side of the grant at moderate cost. The expense of transportation to American or European ports need be no more than freights on lumber from Michigan or Wisconsin to those markets.

Cattle and horses can be raised at an annual cost of thirty cents per head, including interest on purchase price. No disease prevails among them. Beeves grown on this grant can be sold when two years old or older, in Europe, for $10 to $15 more per head than animals of like weight and quality from the United States will bring in those markets at the same time, because cattle from the States must be slaughtered on the docks where unloaded, while those from countries free from pleuro-pneumonia may be taken into the pastures or the stalls for grazing and fattening. There is a strong demand in Europe for such stock.

In healthfulness the north coast of Honduras compares well with the most favored States of the Union. The pure sea air blowing almost constantly from the ocean acts as a bracing tonic, while freedom from swamps prevents the general prevalence of malarial disorders.

CLIMATE, SOIL AND PRODUCTIONS.

CLIMATE.

The climate of Honduras is comparatively cool, and more equable than that of any region in the United States. During the greater part of the year the northeast trade winds, cooled by their passage across the Atlantic ocean and the Caribbean sea, blow over the land, reducing the temperature below that of summer in countries lying farther north. The mean temperature throughout the year for the whole of Honduras has for years been about 74° F. The extreme range has been from 46° F. in remarkably cold winters to 97° F. in exceptionally hot summers. Observations covering a year show that at the mouth of Black river, the extreme range during a year was from 62° to 86° F., a variation of 24°, giving a mean of 74° F. At Caratasca the hottest four months of the year showed a mean temperature of 84°, with a range reaching from 78° to 94°. At Truxillo the mean during the same months was 78° F. This was much lower than the mean temperature of the summer months in States lying east of the Mississippi, and very far below that of the arid western States and Territories, where stock-growing has been for years a profitable business. At Fort Keogh, in Montana, the mercury rose to 135° in the summer of 1887 and in less than six months thereafter sank to 65° below zero, a range of 200° to compare with an extreme range of 51° in the course of years in Honduras. In the mountain regions of the Republic the air is peculiarly clear, pure and bracing, the days made pleasant by breezes sweeping steadily across the mountains, the nights cool enough to make heavy woolen blankets a comfort. In such a climate there is no likelihood of northern people losing whatever energy they may have.

HEALTHFULNESS.

In healthfulness as in climate, the northeastern coast of Hon-

8

duras excels even the most favored States of the Union. Pure
sea breezes, blowing almost constantly over hundreds of miles of
ocean, act as a bracing tonic. There are no swamps to breed
malarial disorders, the little disease of that nature being a mild
type of ague which attacks some of the people who dwell on the
rich alluviums, and neglect all sanitary measures.

The country is absolutely free from many diseases common in
other lands. Scarlet fever, diphtheria, whooping cough, croup,
etc., are unheard of, and yellow fever has never been known
there. Tuberculosis is practically unknown. There is some
catarrh, probably due to the want, among the masses, of com-
fortable dwellings and fires for warming and drying them in the
wet seasons. But although living, as many do, in utter ignorance
of proper sanitary means, and without even the most common
comforts, they are less subject to disease than are the people of
the oldest States of the Union.

Under date of May 28, 1888, Señor Don Dion Galindo, col-
lector of customs for the district of Trujillo, including the De
partment of Colon, certified that:

In this port, and also on the coast of this Department, we have not
had and have not now any infectious or contagious sickness. When we
learn of any such disease in Belize, or in Livingston, quarantine is established in this place. This has kept the people of Trujillo in a state of
perfect health.

T. A. Matute, M.D., a graduate of the University of New
York, registered physician and surgeon of the University of Honduras, and army surgeon at Trujillo until he recently resigned
to go into business for himself, certifies as follows:

There has not been during my six years' experience on this coast, or
in any previous years, any disease of infectious or epidemic character.
There has never been known on all this coast, from Trujillo to Puerto
Cortez, any case of yellow fever or any other epidemic disease, and at
present there is not the slightest reason to fear any infectious diseases.

RAINFALL.

Variations in the configuration of the surface of Honduras
make corresponding differences in the seasons and rainfall in

different parts of the country. On this subject E. G. Squier, Charge d' Affaires of the United States to Central America in 1847, and author of a work which to this day stands the best authority on natural conditions of Honduras, wrote : "The whole of Central America comes within the zone of the northeast trade winds, which sweeping across the Atlantic reach the continent almost saturated with vapor. The portion of moisture of which they are deprived by the Caribbean islands is probably nearly, if not quite, made up in their passage over the sea of the same name. These winds are intercepted by the high mountain centers of the continent, and the vapor precipitated from them flows down to the Atlantic through a multitude of streams and rivers." Again, he says : "For about four months of the year, from May to October, the trades being intermittent, the Pacific declivity is subject to winds from the west and the southwest which precipitate their waters against the western slopes of the mountains, and constitute the rainy season. As these Pacific winds are seldom more than exaggerated sea breezes, and are rarely of more than a few hours' continuance, the rains which follow them are brief, occurring generally in the afternoon and night. It is rare to witness an entire day of rain, although there are occasionally meteoric combinations which produce what the Spaniards call *temporales*, or rain of several days' continuance."

Records of the rainfall of the Republic show that the average annual amount is about forty-eight inches, or the same as that of Central Kentucky and of Savannah, Ga., a little less than that at New Orleans, Baton Rouge, Natchez, Huntsville, Ala., Washington, Ark, Ft. Myer, Va., Ft. Tonson, Ind. Ter., Meadow Valley, Cal. and many other places in the United States. In the most favored parts of the States the average annual rainfall is about the same as in Honduras, while large areas in this country have less.

In the region where the Perry grant is situated the rainfall is distributed over a large part of the year. From May to December showers frequently fall, usually passing quickly, leaving the

sky sunny and the ground watered just enough to force a luxuriant growth of crops. In September and October heavier rains
fall, but even then work can be carried on with little or no more
interruption than usually occurs in the Northern States in October and November. In what is called the wet season there are
often days and sometimes even weeks when no rain falls. As a
whole the worst of the rainy season resembles late autumn weather
in the northeastern States, except that in Mosquitia the temperature never sinks as low as it does in the fall in those States. The
dry season is almost perfect, every day being clear, bright, breezy
and even in temperature. As a winter resort for invalids and
pleasure seekers this coast is unequalled by the best resort known
in the United States, so far as natural advantages are concerned;
and as a summer resort for those who enjoy sea baths, safe yacht-
ing, steady, regular and cooling breezes, fresh fish, terrapin,
green and other turtle steaks, and eggs, a profusion of tropical
fruits and flowers, or deer, boar, jaguar, andante and manatee
hunting, this grant can not be surpassed by any place within
easy disance from the great cities of the United States.

SOIL.

While the soil of this grant is varied in character there is little
if any of it that can not be cultivated much more profitably than
any considerable number of farms in the United States are
worked. Along the ocean is a strip of sandy land from one to
ten miles wide. On this cocoanuts, oranges, mangoes, papayas,
bread fruit, limes and lemons, corn, cane, rice, yams, sweet potatoes, arrowroot, and a great variety of other fruits and vegetables
yield abundantly. There are on the grant fully 120 square miles
of such land, every acre of which can be made, by a minimum
of labor, to give au average yearly profit of $50 to $200, by
planting to cocoanuts alone.   •

Around the lagoons on this grant is an area of land of moderate size which is admirably suited for growing rice, sugarcane,
bananas, plantains, roots and vegetables of many kinds, cotton,
breadfruit, and cocoanuts. At the water's edge these lands are

often no more than 12 to 20 inches above high tide, from which height they gradually slope upward until the prairies are reached. The soil is exceedingly rich, consisting of silt brought down from the mountains and distributed by the rivers. It is not certain that the grant contains land which will yield more sure, abundant and profitable crops than can be grown on these low grounds.

Along the streams are rich alluvial tracts on which valuable woods and medicinal plants abound. Here plantations of fruits yield for years in succession, with no other attention than is required for gathering so much of their products as may be needed for home use. Cleared of the forests which now occupy them, these valleys will support a large population in ease and luxury.

Between these valleys are high and gently undulating prairies or savannas covered by grasses affording pasturage on which stock keep in good condition at all times of the year. Even at the end of the dry season, when the forage might be supposed to have little nutriment, dams suckling their young continue fat. Closely and continuously grazed these plants give way to gramma and other grasses of superior quality. The soil of these prairies is vegetable mold, sand and clay mixed with gravel, and resting on a gravelly subsoil. Pine groves appear at short distances from each other on these savannas.

On the west and in the southern part of the grant are heavily timbered hills. On these the soil is generally loam and vegetable mold. The great size of the mahogany, sapadillo and cedar, liquid amber, locust and other trees of great value, gives ample evidence of the richness of the land.

AN OFFICIAL REPORT.

A few years ago an exploration of Mosquitia was made at the instance of the national Government. The following is a translation of that part of the official report relating to the region of the Perry grant:

The character, or physical appearance, of this part of Mosquitia, is rather monotonous, as it varies but little, being largely extensive plains, extending from the Rio Sico, past the mines of El Dorado and Rio Tinto [Black or Negro River] to Rio Paz toward the south, over an amorphous formation. On the borders of the Paz old and splendid cedars and mahogany trees are found, as well as an extensive growth of fibrous plants. The condition of these lands is excellent for agriculture.

Paon [Black] and Platano rivers flow through the mountain systems bearing their names. Almost all over the Mosquitia region, and especially descending from the south to the sea, hills and mountains disappear and boundless savannas spread on all sides, except where interrupted by river valleys. These are full of trees, including cedar, and mahogany. The ridges of the savannas do not rise more than two metres from the lower soil or general level.

The savannas are generally dry, but as one approaches the coast there are swamps. In the rainy season these sometimes become impassable; but this happens only on lands very close to the coast, and at those times during the rainy season when the rivers overflow low lands. These facts lead to the belief that all of the waters near the coast, from Rio Sico eastward, could be made continuously navigable, it being very easy to connect the rivers with each other by opening small ditches or canals.

Between the Rios Patuca and Ulan the land is all level and sandy, but in the tracts near the rivers excellent and fruitful land is found. Tobacco, rice, beans, corn, coffee, cacao, or anything planted grow beautifully.

In the district of Patuca is found the most beautiful and picturesque part of Mosquitia   There are extensive pampas or plains and spacious lowlands. In the streams fish are abundant. The pasturage of these lands could maintain over 100,000 cattle. There are here ocotals, or groups of pine trees, some of the groups being fifteen to twenty miles wide. Similar ocotals are found at Caratasca. Toward the south of this district, and in the center of it, one may travel five days across savannas and pampas abundantly provided with pure water. Deer, wild pigs, jaquillas, apes, turkeys, pajuils, and a great variety of waterfowl are very tame here. On the margins of the rivers precious woods are very abundant, such as mahogany, cedar, granadillo, ronron, and santa maria, and medicinal plants, as sarsaparilla, ipecacuana, etc., with India-rubber and numberless other useful woods.

Rio Patuca has an average depth of five to seven feet on its bar. From a short distance from the sea to the place where, twenty-four miles up the stream, it divides to send part of its water to Brus lagoon, it is from three to five varas [8½ to 14 feet] deep. From this place, following its course until it joins the Guayambre, in the Department of Olancho, there is always, in the rainy season, from two to five feet of water. From the bar of the Patuca to the mouth of the Guampu navigation is possible.

In April and May last, Mr James P. Taylor made an examination of the Perry grant. He was employed to do this in the interest of a capitalist residing in Tegucigalpa, the capital of the Republic. Mr. Taylor's letters to his employer say, under date of Truxillo, May 4, 1888:

I reached here last evening from Brus lagoon, and as the steamer goes to-day I haven't time to make a full report of all we saw, but will only give the outlines of our trip, and write you fully by the next mail.

On account of our little pack-mule we had to travel very slowly, being unable at any place to hire another. We were until the 10th reaching Dulce Nombre, this being the place designated to leave the Truxillo road and cross the mountains to the grant. But to my disgust we were told by the Indians that we would have to go on foot, as there was no road over which we could take our mules. Being unwilling to give up our mules at this stage of the game we made a trial, but had to abandon them three leagues from the town, sending Fernando with them and a part of our baggage to await our arrival here. So Mr. Perry and I loaded down four Payas with hammocks, blankets, provisions, etc., and started on foot for the river Guampu. We were a little more than two days making it, the distance being about thirty miles. Here we found a pipante, and putting our " traps " and ourselves in it we set sail for the Patuca. Well, we had a rather rough voyage of it, and were wrecked many times before we reached the Patuca.

We were two days on the Guampu; the distance I estimate at about fifty to sixty miles, the last thirty miles of which is through a very pretty little valley, rich and suitable for the growing of bananas, plantains, etc. We saw many growing wild the entire distance of the valley. At Pau river, some twenty miles up the Guampu, the Sumo Indians have a village of some forty or fifty people, the only settlement on the river.

We were on the Patuca four days to Cropunto, where the river makes a big bend to the east, stopping at all the Indian villages as we came down. At Cropunto we crossed the country on foot, southeast to the Guaranta, the east boundary of the grant, and going down that river to the lagoon of the same name, which has an entrance to Carataska. All this country lying between the Patuca and Guaranta rivers is one vast savanna dotted over with ocotals, excepting along the banks of these rivers and other streams. The bush land runs back from one hundred yards to a mile wide, and in places more.

Around all these lakes, Carataska, Guaranta and Brus the land is low, and a portion lying between the Patuca and Carataska is swampy. I mean that portion at which point the Patuca runs within about four miles of the lake; and in the wet season, I am told, pipantes can cross from the lake to within a mile of the river.

Leaving these lakes we returned to Cro punto and embarked in our pipante for Brus on the 24th, reaching there that night. Here we stayed two days awaiting a boat. Then Mr. Perry went back to Caratasca lake, and I started for here, and was six days in making it, three days of which we lay at the entrance of Brus lagoon. The sea being very rough with a north wind, we could not get out with our dory.

Mr. Perry is delighted with the grant, and I assure you he has a right to be. We saw vast bodies of good grazing land, usually well watered, and the cattle, what few we saw, were fat. We were told that nothing in the way of insects troubled either horses or cattle. We saw no snakes, but we were told that in the bush land there are a great many. I found it nothing like as hot as I had expected; although we were walking a great deal we did not suffer from heat. A strong east wind blows from about nine or ten in the morning all day, and the nights are pleasant. We were troubled at a few places by mosquitoes, but this was when we slept on the banks of the rivers.

I will give you a detailed account by the next mail of all we saw, and any opinion I may have. Suffice it to say that in my judgment you have a big thing, and with the proper expenditure of a few hundred thousand you will have a property worth a good sum—I think you could say *millions.* Hope you had a pleasant trip home. We had splendid health all the way, and nothing to complain of except that our "grub" was short a few times. Truly yours,

J. P. TAYLOR.

Under date of May 13, Mr. Taylor wrote again to his employer as follows:

Having traveled from southwest to northeast through the grant, and also across the south and the north ends, we were able to see a great portion of the lands, streams and lakes belonging to the grant. In order to give you an idea of the rivers, lakes, savannas and mountains, I enclose a rough sketch, which will serve to point out the different localties and give you a better idea of the country. Although you will at once discover that I am a poor maker of maps, you will understand the design and overlook my shortcomings.

The Patuca, the largest of any of the rivers, winds its way through the grant from the southwest to the northeast, thus flowing more than 150 miles (all of which is navigable) through the lands of the Honduras Company. Of course it will require some work in the way of cleaning out snags. In one place there are some rocks, and one or two shoals will need channeling a little, but none of the work will be costly, and it will require but little time to have it in good condition for boats.

The grant being divided by the Patuca river, we have on the east, or or rather on the southeast, a vast scope of savanna or ocotal, broken only by the spurs of the Juticalpa mountains in the extreme south, running down a few miles. On and around these the Sumo Indians gather considerable rubber, sarsaparilla, etc. On these savanna lands grow the common wild grasses of this country, on which the cattle and horses seem to thrive, and, although it is now late in the dry season, they are fat and look better than any we saw in the Olancho country. Nothing seems to trouble either cattle or horses, and while in places you find the grass a little thin, and such places will require some acreage, you nevertheless find sufficient good grazing lands on this side of the river for many thousands of head of stock. The savanna or ocotal lands are separated from the river by skirts of bush land which is from nothing to a few miles wide. This bush land, which is almost like a jungle, is what the natives raise their bananas, etc., on.

The Guaranta river on the east, as far up as we were, ten to fifteen miles, is very crooked, has but little fall, and the banks are low. The lands lying around Guaranta and Caratasca lagoons are low and in places swampy, so much so that I do not think it would be a healthy location for a town or settlement; but these lands are fine for cocals, etc. The swampy parts of these lands fall mostly between the Patuca river and Guaranta lake. From the best information we could gather, it would not cost a great deal to connect them by a canal some four miles long. There being plenty of water in both Caratasca and Guaranta, I should think, for almost any size steamer, and an excellent harbor, I believe this connection to be almost indispensable. At Cropunto we have a beautiful savanna country, this being about a league up the river from where a connection would be made. Here we have plenty of timber for building, good water, etc., making an excellent place for a village or settlement. You can readily see the advantage of a canal, as Brus lagoon has not sufficient water in the channel for anything but small boats; and the bar of the Patuca has less.

We found on this, the southeast side of Patuca, seven Indian villages, estimated to be about 200 in population. Some of them speak a little English; they are strong, active and somewhat industrious, being engaged most of the time in getting rubber, sarsaparilla, etc.

On the northwest side of the Patuca we have the Guampu, Guineo and other streams running into the Patuca. Black river goes to Ebon lake, and Plantain river to the sea. Between the Patuca and Plantain, after you get a short distance back from Brus lake and the sea, you have a large scope of savanna country.* Up all the rivers you have the

*Of this stretch of country lying between the Patuca and Plantain rivers Consul Burchard says: "I have walked for days in succession across the most beautiful savannas there. No better grazing land can be found any where;" and the Government exploring party reports that "and in the center of it one may travel five days across the savannas

finest agricultural lands I have ever seen. You can hardly imagine anything but what will grow most luxuriantly: bananas, plantains, pineapples, sweet potatoes, corn, beans, tomatos, watermelons, and, in fact, almost anything you plant.

All along the coast and around the lagoons, while it is not so good for bananas and plantains, it is so much the better for cocals [cocoanut plantations]; and while anything in the vegetable line grows here it is not so good for bananas, etc., as the soil is sandy, and they don't seem to last many years.

Black river is said to be navigable eighty miles. Ebon lake is fifteen miles long, and extends west within half-a-mile of Plantain river, which is navigable for forty miles. Thus you see that most all of the whole grant is easily reached.

I believe this is as good, if not the best fruit-growing country on this, the north coast of Honduras, and for stock-raising, everything considered, I believe it would be hard to find a place to equal this.

We were told that there are about the same number of Indians on this side of the Patuca as there are on the southeast side. They are all peaceable, and we had no difficulty in getting on all right with them.

We are told that up the Guaranta, Guineo, Black and Plantain there are good lots of mahogany and cedar. I am especially delighted with the Patuca country. While it is a good, large river, it has a strong current and high banks, and overflows but little land even at its highest. I think it is perfectly healthy; usually a good strong breeze blows from morning to night.

The route from Juticalpa to the river Patuca, via Dulce Nombre, Lagarto, and Guampu is perfectly practicable for a wagon road, which can be made at reasonable cost. The whole distance from the mouth of the Guampu to Juticalpa is about 150 miles, twenty-six leagues of which would be through the Juticalpa valley, and would require but little work. The Lagarto section would be the most difficult, as it is mountainous and, like the Guampu, has a heavy undergrowth; but I think we have sufficient scope to get a good, easy grade, and as the subsoil is of a sandy nature, by cutting the timber well away from the road I think it would be reasonably dry at all seasons of the year.

Taking the grant as a whole, I think it is decidedly a very fine piece of property, and while I believe thoroughly in some of the mines of

and pampas abundantly provided with pure water." See page 13. Reporting to the general Government in reply to questions about this grant, Senor Fernando Martinez, governor of Colon, said, November 4, 1887: "The lands referred to contain a number of mountains covered with every kind of woods, India rubber, cactus and pita fibres, and so extensive and unobstructed savannas that the view is lost in the distance."

2

Honduras I know of none that I would like to exchange the "tiger ranch" for. This may seem a bold assertion, but when you see it and have traveled over it, I think you are not too much prejudiced in favor of minerals to agree with me.

CABINET AND OTHER WOODS.

The more valuable of the woods found on the Perry grant are mahogany, lignumvitae, rosewood, algarroba, ebony, yellow sandal-wood, cedar, India-rubber, cypress, santa maria, sapadillo, laurel, pole-wood or granadillo, sapote, several kinds of oak and a great variety of palms. Of some of these the texture is very fine, and capable of receiving a fine polish. For the lumber made from them ready sale can doubtless be always found at fair profits. Of the mahogany, E. G. Squier said in his "Notes on Central America:"

The mahogany grows in nearly all parts of Honduras, in the valleys of the various streams. It is, however, most abundant upon the low grounds which border the rivers flowing into the Bay of Honduras, where it also attains its greatest size and beauty, and where the mahogany-works, called "cortes" (cuttings) by the Spaniards, are chiefly confined. As these lands are for the most part the property of the State, the wood is cut under licenses obtained from the government, which exacts a fixed sum for each tree. Except those made at the mouth of the various rivers for receiving, marking and shipping the wood as it floated down, the mahogany establishments are necessarily temporary, and changed from time to time as trees become scarce in their neighborhood.

Writing of the pine, the cedar and the ceiba, Squier said, in the same work:

Among the common and most useful woods, the long-leaved or pitch pine deserves the first mention, not less on account of its excellent quality than its great abundance. It may almost be said to cover all the more elevated portions of Honduras, from one sea to the other. Upon the Pacific slope of the continent it makes its appearance on the hills and mountains at the height of about 1,200 feet above the sea. Toward the interior it is found at lower elevations, and on the Atlantic declivity it is abundant nearly down to the sea level. I found it on the low hills bordering the great plain of Sula, on the west, at the height of 250 feet; and it is well known that on the savannas bordering the rivers and lagoons to the eastward of Truxillo, as well as on the Mosquito Shore, it is a characteristic feature. The trees do not grow closely together, but stand well apart, permitting the mountain grasses to grow beneath and around them, so that a pine forest in the interior more resembles a well-kept park than the thickets to which we are accustomed to give the name of forest. The trees grow frequently to great size, but average about twenty inches in diameter. They are rich in pitch, and the wood is firm, heavy, and durable, and the heart is never attacked by insects. It furnishes, therefore, a cheap and convenient timber for all kinds of constructions in the country, as well for bridges as for buildings and for boats. Captain Henderson observes of the Honduras pine; "The timber which it furnishes can scarcely be exceeded in size, and is generally considered, for every necessary purpose, greatly superior to what can be imported from the United States;" and Strangeways expresses the conviction that the endless tracts of pine forest on the northern coast will ultimately come to furnish a large supply both of pitch, tar, and timber for the wants of commerce.

The cedro, or cedar (Cedrela Odorata, L.), ranks next to the pine in the list of common and useful woods. It is found in all the valleys, but more particularly in those of the principal rivers near the coast. It attains the height of seventy or eighty feet, and a diameter of from four to seven feet. It is not attacked by insects, is light and easily worked, as well as ornamental in color and agreeable in smell. For these reasons, it is more extensively used than any other wood in Honduras. It is now exported in small, but increasing quantities. Most of the canoes and pitpans of the natives are hollowed from the trunks of the cedro, and are both light and durable, but liable to be split in beaching.

The ceiba, or silk-cotton-tree (Bombax Ceiba, L.), is abundant, and distinguished for its vast size, which leads to its common use for ' bongos ' and ' pitpans.' I have seen boats, hollowed from a single trunk, which would measure seven feet in ' the clear' between the sides. This tree blossoms two or three times a year, when its carnation flowers give a bloom to an entire forest. It produces a pod containing a kind of downy fibre or cotton, which is sometimes used to stuff cushions and pillows, and may possibly be made useful for other purposes.

The larger of the mahogany trees which grew within easy distance from the Patuca were cut, many years ago, by English and by Scotch companies. They left the other valuable woods almost untouched. In the long time which has passed since those companies abandoned the field the timber has improved so greatly in size that the ground might be profitably cut over again, even though no other wood than mahogany should be taken. The cedar, rosewood, santa maria, sapadillo and other fine woods in the valley will of themselves pay large profits. Native laborers can be hired at wages ranging from $8 to $15 a month, and rations. The Patuca is a stream down which logs can be driven with ease and safety, and at small cost. The Guaranta, Plantain, Secre, Pimento, Guineo and other rivers have not been occupied by timber cutters. Each of these streams can be worked profitably.

The Hon. Wm. C. Burchard, United States consul at Ruatan, has lived thirty-three years in Honduras. During several of those years he was Governor of the Department of Mosquitia, in which the Perry grant is included, and which now forms a large part of the Department of Colon. In this long period Mr. Burchard has accumulated the knowledge which gives him the reputation of being more fully and accurately informed about northern Honduras than is any other man. From personal observation he is able to furnish complete and valuable information about all parts of Mosquitia, its natural productions and its capabilities. From his letter-book the subjoined extracts from a letter written in June, 1879, are taken :

The forests of Mosquitia are without doubt richer in fine-grain woods than those of any other Department of this Republic. Princely fortunes have been made by English speculators in mahogany, on some of the rivers in the province. The rivers Segovia and Patuca have been worked for many years on a very large scale. At present the largest mahogany works are those of the river Aguan. * * * * At present all the lumber and furniture used in Spanish and in British Honduras are imported from the United States. The duty here on imported furniture is eight cents a pound.

From the foregoing facts and from your personal observations in this country, it will be an easy matter for you to make a very reliable estimate of the magnitude of the business and of the profit which might be realized from a sawmill and furniture factory to supply the demand in Truxillo, Puerto Cortes, San Pedro, Omoa, the Bay Islands and the British colony of Belize, as well as for export to the United States. The Plantain river, the Sico, Limoncito and the Secre have never been worked, and are said to be rich in mahogany.

In another letter dated September 8, 1879, Consul Burchard

wrote in reply to questions forwarded from the Department of State:

Honduras is a mountainous country, drained by a number of large rivers fed by rapid tributaries, many of wh'ch are natural water-powers capable of running mills of almost any capacity. They can be secured, not only without cost, but I think that the local authorities of the large towns would give material aid toward the establishment of saw-mills and other kinds of machinery, which are greatly needed by the country. Such establishments would pay best in the interior, especially in the rich Department of Olancho, where lumber, furniture, wagons, carts, carriages etc., would find a ready market, and where northern men can enjoy a most delicious climate, and surround themselves, by a little industry, with all the comforts and luxuries of both temperate and tropical zones.

There is little or no need of calling attention to the advantages which will result to Honduras and to any persons or company through supplying this demand. Those advantages will become more plainly apparent when a good wagon road shall have been constructed to connect the north coast with the interior of the Republic. The opening of such a road from the head of navigation to the city of Juticalpa, the capital of the rich Department of Olancho, will enable such a company to furnish, at lower prices than have ever been known there, all the lumber and furniture which will be needed in the great valley system of which Juticalpa is naturally the commercial center.

The north coast of Honduras alone uses from 2,000,000 to 3,000,000 feet of pine lumber in a year, and the Bay Islands from 150,000 to 250,000 feet per annum. Mill-run long-leaved pine, unplaned sells for $35, and planed for $45 per M. All the lumber used on the coast of the Carribean sea, from Yucatan in the north, to Venezuela in the south is imported, chiefly from Nova Scotia and the United States. The consumption will increase as great public works will be undertaken in Central America, and as the people of other lands learn something of the advantages these sub-tropical countries offer to enterprise and capital. This increased demand this grant will, by reason of its favorable geographical position, excellent harbor and other advantages, be able to supply at fair prices from its almost inexhaustible forests.

FRUITS AND THE FRUIT TRADE.

Of fruits Honduras produces a large variety, which find ready sale at home, as well as in the markets of other lands. Chief among these in commercial, as in food value, are bananas. Of these there are several kinds, the most valued being the platano or plantain. All through the country these are an important part of the daily food of the people. Along the north coast of the Republic quantities of bananas and plantains are grown, principally for the markets of the United States. Within the last ten years the traffic in this fruit and others on this coast has grown so largely that three lines of steamers find regular employment in carrying the crops to the North. Yet all this trade has been, and is now confined to that part of the coast beginning seventy miles from the western boundary of the grant, and extending to Guatemala.

A plan often recommended by planters in Honduras is to set banana or plantain sprouts fifteen feet apart, making 193 plants to the acre. Each of these plants will yield a bunch of fruit in about nine months after planting. These sell on the coast for prices ranging at different times from $37\frac{1}{2}$ to 75 cents, and sometimes, although rarely, for $1, and even for $1.25 each. This gives from $72 to $240 for the first crop from an acre. After that the yield is larger, as two to four of the young sprouts which spring up around the parent stock are permitted to grow and bear. Estimates as to the cost of planting and caring for plantations of bananas or of plantains differ in various parts of tropical America. In some localities in Central America, and under systems of management followed by many, the cost is from $20 to $25 a manzana of 10,000 square yards, or two acres. One of the latest and most conservative estimates is that which was printed February 18, 1888, in *El Diario Nicaraguense*, of Granada, Nicaragua. It states that its estimate was published to correct another, made public by the Commissioner of the Mosquito Reserve, which latter estimate is characterized by *El Diario* as being " pessimistic, exaggerated, extravagant, and calculated to mislead the public. "

The Mosquito Reserve lies next south of the Republic of Honduras. The estimate of *El Diario* states that the cost of preparing the land, planting and caring for 44½ manzanas, or 92 acres, and the income therefrom are as follows:

Outlay First Year.

44½ manzanas or 92 acres, and clearing the same	$ 3,115
10,000 sprouts, @ 1c. each...............	100
Cultivating, first year, @ $12 per manzana...................... ..	534
Wages and sustenance of manager................................	708
Wages eight extra laborers, 15 days harvesting fruit.............	64
Food for eight laborers, 15 days @ 30c per diem each....	36
Wages and food for cook @ $23 per month......................	276
Building utensils, etc., etc...	1,000
Total cost.......·.........	$ 5,833

Income.

12,000. bunches @ 50c gold.....................		$ 6,000
Premium on gold @ 33 per cent.............		1,980
Total,		$ 7,980
Deduct 20 per cent for fruit lost, ...	$ 1,596	
Deduct cost as shown above,.........................	5,833—	7,429
Net gains.................................		$ 551

Outlay Second Year.

Wages 8 laborers @ $16 per month......	$ 1,536
Food for 8 men @ 30 c. each per diem	876
Wages and food of manager and cook	984
Materials, replanting and incidental expenses...................	500
Total cost.....,.......................	$ 3,896

Income.

30,000 bunches @ 50c. gold,.......		$15,000
Premium on gold @ 33 per cent...................		4,950
Total...		$19,950
Deduct 20 per cent. for fruit lost......	$ 3,900	
Deduct cost as above for second year............. ...	3,896—	7,886
Net profits second year................ ... .$		12,064

In 1879 Consul W. C. Burchard wrote on the subject of growing bananas and plantains in the Province of Mosquitia, where this grant is located, as follows ;

I believe that facts and figures will warrant me in saying that there is no agricultural labor more profitable, in relation to the capital required, than that of cultivating bananas and some other tropical fruits in this country. I will give you the cost and product of a manzana (100 yards square) of land planted with bananas:

Cost of clearing the land	$10 00
750 sprouts	7 50
Planting 750 sprouts or suckers	10 00
Cultivating until first crop is harvested	15 00
Interest on investment one year	4 25
Total	**$46 75**

This plantation the first year, or probably in ten months after planting the suckers, will yield 750 bunches of bananas, which at the present price of seventy-five cents each here will give $562, or a net profit of $515.75 on an investment, with interest added, of $46.75. So much for the first year. For the second, and if the land is good, for twenty succeeding years, the said plantation of 100 yards square will give an annual product (according to soil) of from two to four times as much as that of the first year. The only expense after the first harvest would be to clear out the weeds once a year (about $10), and that of cutting and delivering the fruit to vessels, which would be from six to ten cents for each bunch.

Of course there are drawbacks to this, as to almost all other kinds of farming. No crop is more certain than that of bananas. The great, and I believe the only enemy to the fruit planter in Honduras, is the north wind. In the winter months we sometimes have heavy gales, northers, which uproot the banana trees which are not protected by hills or by forest trees, and a partial loss of the crop is the consequence. But only the fruit suffers. The tree is never killed, as, whether it is standing or lying on the ground, new suckers will always come up from the roots.

The province of Mosquitia has as yet exported no fruit, although no other part of the country possesses as many advantages for its production. Bananas grow spontaneously, and attain the highest degree of perfection on the margins of all its principal rivers, and afford an inexhaustible supply of food for monkeys, parrots and other wild denizens of the forest. Plantain river, which derives its name from the abundance of wild bananas and plantains which grow spontaneously on its banks and in its valleys, is worthy of especial attention, offering as it does, a large and certain supply of fruit, equal to the best in the country, [which is secured to us by our grant from the Government], and which can be made immediately a source of revenue. These banana groves are first seen about thirty-five miles up the Plantain river from its mouth, and from thence further up for a distance of about thirty miles, the river, on both sides, is almost one continuous banana plantation, a narrow border of trees on either bank, which occasionally extend a considerable distance back into the bottom lands. It is difficult to make anything like an accurate estimate of the amount of fruit suitable for the shipment which might be obtained from Plantain river alone, but it is quite safe to calculate that a steamship capable of carrying 8,000 to 10,000 bunches, could be loaded there every month. By having a little steamboat to tow barges up and down the river, I am satisfied that the cost of cutting the fruit and delivering it alongside of the shipping would not exceed twelve and one-half cents a bunch.

Later, the Consul wrote to a company which proposed to engage in the fibre business in Mosquitia: "Facts and figures will warrant me in saying that, by an expenditure of $3,000 to $5,000, the banana fields of Plantain river will alone yield the company a net profit of ten per cent. on the amount of its capital stock [$600,000]." Of the quality of this fruit Mr. Burchard wrote last year: "It is larger and better than most of the bananas grown in cultivated fields."

In relation to these fields of wild fruit Mr. Wm. H. McKee, who examined this region in 1882 in the interest of the company mentioned, wrote:

The fruit-growing privileges of Plantain river can be understood only by being seen. The soil is of that quality most desirable for the production of bananas, and the banks subject to that gentle inundation which is considered to be of all things the most beneficial to a banana plantation, and which certainly renders the never-failing fertility of the soil assured.

From just above the mouth of the river, for the space of a day and a half's journey, the banks of the river for a space of from a few rods to a mile and a half upon either side, are clear of forests, covered only by a rank growth of grass, wild cane and bananas.

The Mosquito Indians say that in former times the king of the Mosquitans chose the banks of this river as the site for an immense plantation, and each year compelled his subjects to clear and plant a certain area, which course being followed for a long period of years resulted in this extensive clearing, which has never again grown up to forests, but remains to this day a natural plantation, requiring only the proper care to produce fruit enough to freight a fleet.

Plantains and bananas are found growing wild on the banks of other streams on this grant, especially on the Patuca and the Guineo, so named because guineos (bananas) abound along its borders, as they do to a less extent near other waters here. At moderate cost these uncared-for patches of fruit may be extended

until they will occupy a tract as wide as the crop can be profitably carried over to the boats, and along the entire length of the
navigable waters of these rivers and lagoons. They will be a
source from which supplies of sprouts can be obtained at nominal cost, for many years.

Some idea of the rapidity of the growth which the fruit trade
of northern Honduras made, even in the earlier years of its ex-
istence, is given by another extract from a letter previously quoted
on page 24. The writer said :

During the last eighteen months the trade in tropical fruits between
Honduras and the United States has grown to a wonderful extent, and
is constantly and rapidly increasing. Reference to the consular reports
of this office will give you many interesting facts and figures in regard
to our trade with Honduras. In the register of arrivals and departures
of American vessels you will find that since the first of January last to
the first of this month, June, there have been fifty-one arrivals of American vessels from ports of the United States to this port of Ruatan.
This does not include the arrivals at Truxillo, Puerto Cortes and Utilla,
which ports belong to this consular district. Of the said fifty-one arrivals, twenty-one were steamships and thirty sailing vessels. The in-
voice book shows that for the same period, viz., five months, exports of
fruits from this port to the United States have been as follows: 164,000
bunches of bananas, 1,124,000 coconuts, 1,053,000 plantains, besides pro-
portionate quantities of pineapples, limes, oranges, mangoes, tamarinds,
some India rubber, sarsaparilla, hides, deerskins, etc., etc. Imports from
the United States consist of flour, provisions, lumber, furniture, petro-
leum, hardware, boots and shoes, lager beer, tobacco, drygoods, etc.

Great as the growth of the trade in bananas has been, it will
probably be surpassed by that of the traffic in plantains when the
people of the United States shall have had opportunity to learn
the food value of the last named fruit. There are several varieties of the plantains, some of which are dried and preserved, in
which condition they will keep twenty-five or thirty years. Flour
from plantains is made into nutritive biscuits. Of the fresh fruit
100 parts contain twenty-seven parts of dry nutritive matter, or
only two parts less than the potato. A single plant bears from
twenty-five to ninety pounds of fruit, worth $7.50 per 1,000 single
fruits, or three-fourths cent each. An acre will bear 435 plants,

which, averaging seventy pounds of fruit each, will yield 30,450 pounds of nutritive matter and some 600 pounds of fibre. The returns from plantains will be found to be fully as large as those from bananas, while the demand will be stronger and more constant. At present the people of those United States ports where plantains are landed, buy all that are offered, so that none reach interior towns. The fruit is cooked in a great number of ways, and in all stages of growth. Dogs, cattle, horses, pigs, fowls and almost all other animals eat the banana and the plantain. To a large degree this fruit takes the place of breadstuffs in all countries in which it grows.

A person can start from New Orleans or Mobile with only $275 in his pocket, and by planting bananas on this grant can in one year begin to get an income of $1,800 per annum. His fare to the coast will be $35; clearing and planting 10 acres, $120; expenses of living, $120; total, $275. He can himself clear and plant 10 acres at least, making a total of 20 acres of plantation which will each yield 200 bunches for the first crop, 9 months after planting, or a total of 4,000 bunches. During eight months of the year the price will be about 50 cents a bunch. At those figures the crop would bring $2.000. For four months the price is about 35 cents a bunch, which would give an income of $1,400 each nine months.

Pineapples grow to large size, and of superior flavor in North-eatern Honduras. The variety known as sugar pines is especially worthy of attention, being very large and sweet. On the sandy land between Caratasca lagoon and the ocean they often reach a circumference of 17½ to 18 inches, by 27 to 30 inches in the longer circumference, and a weight of 5 to 7 pounds.

In some places pineapple sprouts are planted in rows 3½ feet apart, the plants being set 2½ feet apart in the rows. This gives 4,080 to the acre from which 4,000 pines should be obtained in 16 to 18 months after planting. In the Bahamas the plants are permitted to grow within 18 inches of each other, making 19,360 to to an acre, but the yield is probably neither as good in quality

nor as large in number as from fields in which the plants are farther apart, and in which $25 to $30 per acre is spent per annum
in cultivation.

The usual price for common pineapples on the Honduras
coast is six and one-fourth cents each. The large, sweet sugar
pines will bring at least ten to fifteen cents each when supplied
in quantities great enough to make it an object to keep them
separate from the others in handling. A crop of 4,000 pines at
six and one-fourth cents will bring $240, a net profit of fully
$200 per acre.   If the plants are only eighteen inches apart they
should yield at least 10,000 saleable fruits for the sixteen to eighteen months, worth $625, of which $575 should be net gain which
is equal to $385 for a year, per acre.

Oranges are grown here in profusion, with no care. The
trees are seedlings, untrimmed, and the ground they stand on is
never cultivated—the truth that no land is ever cultivated in this
Republic should be kept in mind. Yet most of the orange trees
there produce good crops of a fair quality and size, and some
yield fruit of exceeding sweetness, and larger than the average
of oranges offered in northern markets.

A great variety of indigenous and other fruits can be grown
in Honduras, and be profitably sent to foreign markets in a fresh,
or in some preserved form.   To those now grown may be added,
with little labor or expense, apricots, plums, peaches, almonds,
olives, figs, dates, walnuts, etc.   These will become a source of
daily and very large income to cultivators of the lands of Mosquitia.

In " Notes on Honduras," Squire gives a partial list of indigenous fruits of this region.   On page 182 he remarks:

Apart from the lime, lemon, orange, and palm trees, there is a great
variety of trees bearing fruits which are indigenous in the country.
The cacao is one of these, and is remarkably abundant on the northern alluvions, where the natives draw their entire supplies from the
forests. It is known there as the cacao mico, monkey or wild cacao,
and is distinguished from the cultivated variety by having larger nuts,
and, it is claimed, a finer flavor. The pimento-tree, closely resembling
the Jamaica "allspice" (Myrtus Pimenta), is also indigenous. Its berry

is somewhat larger than the variety found in the islands, but weaker in its aroma, and has not yet entered into the commerce of the country.

The Anona, of several varieties, is also indigenous; the Aguacate, or Alligator Pear (Persea Gratimima); Citron (Citrus Tuberosa); Tamarind (Tamarindus Occidentalis); Guava (Psidium Guajavas); Pines (Bromelia Ananas); Mango (Mangofera Domestica); Papaya (Carica Papaya); Zapote Granado (Punica Granatum); Mamay (Lucuma Bomplandi); Nance; Jocote, or wild Plum ; Manzanilla, etc., etc.

The Vanilla (Epidendrum Vanilla) occurs in the same district with the sarsaparilla, and is remarkable for its luxuriance and the size of its pod. It has not yet become an article of export, but the specimens which have been sent to the United States and Europe have already elicited orders beyond the capacity of the available labor of the coast to supply.

In nearly all parts of Honduras wild guava trees abound. In the region drained by the Patuca and its tributaries, particularly in the valley of Juticalpa, thousands of bushels of guavas ripen each year, only to be eaten by wild animals or to rot on the ground. A large part of this yield might be profitably made to contribute to the earnings of the people of these valleys, by providing means for its easy and quick transportation to factories where this now waste product could be preserved. This is also true of a large variety of indigenous fruits which would sell readily in other countries. Coffee and cacao grow well even on the coast, and require nothing more than ordinary attention to make them very profitable to the producer.

OTHER INDUSTRIES.

Fruit-growing absorbs the attention of many who learn of the natural resources of northern Honduras; but other industries can be carried on there with as great gains as are obtained from fruits, or even greater. Sarsaparilla from Honduras has for many years been recognized as the best in the markets. By judicious management it can be made to yield 1,500 to 2,000 pounds of roots per acre per annum. At rates current on the coast, this is equal to $575 to $700 per acre. By the adoption of better methods in handling the roots, their value will be increased until this crop will become the source of immense revenue to settlers on this grant.

Plantations of ule, or India-rubber trees, pay richly. The systematic cultivation of rubber trees has been fairly tested, and the field is new and a most promising one.

The greater part of the income of the Indians who live in Mosquitia comes through the gathering of rubber, sarsaparilla, liquid amber, copal and other products of forest and plain; but the Indians are so very few, and the quantity of gums, roots and plants used in the arts or in medicine is so great, that these may be made to give employment and good pay to all who will gather them. Some at least may be cultivated profitably. Reference to the very incomplete list of natural productions of this region, given on page 56, will give some idea of the variety of such plants found in Mosquitia.

Rice grows well in Honduras, the low lands around the sounds or lagoons being especially adapted to its successful cultivation. Honduras rice sells for better prices than are paid for rice grown in the Southern States. It is sought for seed.

Cotton grows into trees 20 feet high, which yield good staple year after year.

Besides those mentioned, there are other sources of income which will give to settlers on this grant from 200 to 400 per cent. per annum on the capital required for the development and management of such enterprises. Some of them are such as can be carried on profitably in temperate zones, but the greater number and most profitable are of a kind which can never be in competition with the products of regions where frosts occur. The settler need not raise those crops which can be grown in the United States, for he can afford to import flour, corn and calicoes produced in the north by the aid of machinery and underpaid toil, and devote his attention to raising those things which bring high prices, cost a minimum of toil and thought, and can not be grown in very large accessible areas.

In the western end of the grant are deposits of gold, which are known to be rich. East of the Black river mountains lies the Perry grant, which Consul Burchard once described as "a vast unexplored region, inhabited only by uncivilized Indians, which we know contains gold, from the fact that the Indians are constantly bringing small quantities of that precious metal to barter with traders on the coast for ammunition, trinkets, etc. On the west fork of the Tinto [Black River], called Rio Sico, gold is found in the river and all its tributaries, but is extracted only by Indians, and in the rudest manner possible. The only tools they employ are a pointed stick, a horn spoon and a wooden bowl or batea. The mineral wealth of La Mosquitia is yet undeveloped. The few tests that have been made at El Dorado, have given most satisfactory and promising results."

Useful and valuable fibers are obtained from the husk of the cocoanut, from pita plants and from the stalks of bananas, plantain and other growths. From an acre of banana stalks about 600 pounds of fiber can be gathered. Pita fiber is for some uses superior to all others known, and there is no doubt that in a short time all the difficulties which now prevent its general introduction for those uses will be removed.

STOCK-GROWING.

Those who have become thoroughly acquainted with the business of stock-growing in America, and have seen the country in which the Perry grant is situated, agree with the opinion expressed by Mr. Taylor, who says, " for stock-raising, everything considered, I believe it would be hard to find a place equal to this." Several kinds of grasses afford good pasturage in Honduras. The savannas of the northeastern part are covered by forage. In the dry months some of the grasses ripen and cure as they stand, thus making good hay even while there is a growth of green and palatable leaves at the roots of the plants.

Chief in the list of cultivated plants used for forage are maize, Egyptian corn, barley, sugar cane and para grass. The cane is an indigenous variety, softer and richer than the Asiatic kind grown in the United States, and is therefore better as food for stock than the latter would be. The Honduras cane grows continuously without replanting. Cattle eat the leaves and fruit of the banana with avidity. Two crops of maize are grown in a year, and there is no apparent reason why three crops per annum can not be raised from one field. Para grass yields very heavy crops, and is greatly relished by cattle and horses.

Evenness of the temperature, an almost unbroken succession of sunny days throughout the greater part of the year, cooling breezes which blow nearly every day, freedom from annoying insects and other disturbing causes, and an abundance of pure water in every part of the grant, make this tract of country superior to even the most favored part of the ranching region of the United States, where great fortunes were made in cattle-growing before that country became overstocked.

Even under the crude and wasteful method, or lack of method, which has been common on the western plains of the United States, the average annual increase of herds of cattle has equalled 50 per cent. of the number of breeding cows in those herds. This being true of the arid, sun-scorched and blizzard swept plains, what may not be done in Honduras, where cold storms are never known, and where nearly every square league has at least one pure stream, fed by mountain springs. On the northeast coast these flow in gravelly or sandy beds, across plateaus where nutritious grasses are always green. The value of such a copious supply of never-failing water is shown in strong light by the enormous losses caused by want of water last year among live stock in the western States. Favored by all natural conditions, the stock-grower in Honduras can easily get an average annual increase of 75 per cent. in his herds, and can, by careful management, raise the production to 90 per cent. per annum. Horses should give nearly as large a percentage of increase as is obtained from cattle. Cows with their calves beside them, as good in size and quality as the common or "native" stock of the States, can be bought in Honduras for prices ranging from $9 to $12 per head; two-year old heifers sell for $5 to $7, and yearlings at $2.50 to $4. The heifers are usually three years old before they drop their first calves. The cost of managing a herd in northeastern Honduras, where wages are low and the cost of rations for laborers is small, is only a fraction of that of maintaining a herd of like number in the most favored parts of the western States and Territories.

A conservative estimate of the results which can be reached in cattle growing on this grant is presented in the subjoined table. In this calculation it is assumed that of a herd of cows 60 per cent. will each year produce young that will reach marketable age and condition, that half of the bulls born in the herd will be sold when three years old, and the money received for them will be paid for cows to add to the herd. In ten years, 1,000 cows, their offspring and the cows bought with the money received for the bulls would produce as below:

Years.	Breeding cows.	Bulls born.	No. bulls sold.	Av'age value of bulls.	Total value of bulls sold.	No. cows bought.	Av. prices cows bought.
1	1,000	300	150	$15.00	$ 2,250	225	$10.00
2	1,000	300	150	15.00	2,250	225	10.00
3	1,000	300	150	15.00	2,250	225	10.00
4	1,525	457	228	20.00	4,560	415	11.00
5	2,050	615	307	20.00	6,140	558	11.00
6	2,575	772	386	20.00	7,720	643	12.00
7	3,447	1,034	517	25.00	12,925	1,077	12.00
8	4,620	1,386	693	25.00	17,325	1,238	14.00
9	6,035	1,810	905	30.00	27,150	1,810	15.00
10	8,146	2,444	1,222	30.00	36,666	2,037	18.00
Totals	8,146	9,418	4,708	$25.32	$119,230	8,453	$14.10

Assuming that the bulls not sold to pay for cows will be used for breeding, or sold to pay expenses of the herd, the account should stand as shown below, at the end of the first ten years.

1,000 superannuated cows, original herd, at $10.................$ 10,000
7,146 breeding cows, mostly grades, average value say $25....... 178,650
2,772 grade two-year-old bulls and heifers, at $25................. 79,300
3,620 high grade yearling bulls and heifers, at $20.... 72,400
4,888 high grade calves, at $15.................................... 73,320

Total. $413,670

The above estimate allows $119,230 to pay for the expenses of the herd, to provide bulls of high breeding, and to cover deterioration of the breeding cows for ten years. Better results than those shown can be realized on this grant, where all conditions are so favorable, and no possible combination of other interests can tax the producer unduly for transportation, for slaughtering or for selling his stock. As long as the ocean is free to the vessels of all nations there will be competition enough to keep charges down to reasonable limits.

As no fatal contagious disease has ever appeared among the cattle of Honduras, the stock-grower can send his yearlings, two-year-olds and older unfattened bullocks direct to the pastures of Europe. This will give him from $10 to $15 per head more for his stock than like cattle from the United States would bring on the same market. This would in itself amount to a large profit.

While it is true that the raising of cattle will pay richly, the growing of horses and mules on the grant will pay better. All the conditions of soil, configuration, climate, forage, and geographical location are most favorable. Horses and mules raised on thoroughly drained, gravelly or rocky soil, particularly if it be hilly or mountainous, are more muscular, hardy, active and courageous than are those brought up in a flat country. Mountain horses and mules are more highly esteemed than are those from level lands. Their hoofs and bones are finer, harder, and tougher than those of stock grown on moist ground and their form better developed.

Many of the horses of Honduras retain traces of the characteristics of the Arabian stock from which they no doubt descended through animals taken by the Moors to Spain. They are rather small, clean of limb, hard and tough of hoof, and have fine spirit and intelligence with a gentle disposition. They are active and good tempered even under the harsh usage to which horses and mules are commonly subjected by the natives. They have not been used for hard work as much as they would

have been had not mules been generally preferred for such service, yet they still show considerable power of endurance. As
a rule they are larger than the mustangs of the southwest. The
chief value of the mares will be found in their use as foundation
stock from which to breed animals of the Morgan type—active,.
bright and good tempered family horses. Grades got by Cleve-
land bays, French coach, or other horses of like size and style
would sell freely for general use, and would beyond a doubt be
sought for cavalry service, while the get by stallions of the
heavier draft breeds would be desirable for artillery and for team-
ing in cities.

Mares of fair size and quality can be bought in Honduras for
$10 to $12 each. The cost of establishing and managing a stud
in Honduras need not be nearly as great as that of keeping a
stud of like numbers in any part of the States. As the mares are
healthy and perfectly sound, accustomed to taking care of themselves and their foals, and will never suffer from lack of food or
water, nor from exposure to storms, they may be confidently expected to breed surely and well. Probably fully seventy five per
cent. of a stud of such mares would each year produce foals
which would sell for an average of at least $75 each when four
years old. By using stallions of high breeding and uniform size,
style and color, selected as far as practicable from one family, a
large number of almost perfectly matched spans would be got
each year from a stud of say 1,000 such mares as can be bought
in Honduras. From the grade fillies which would come of the
use of such a lot of stallions a large percentage of the foals will
match very closely, and would bring higher prices than un-
matched spans would. The results which can be obtained by
proper management are approximately indicated by the subjoined
estimate, based on the assumption that of a stud of mares sixty
per cent. will each year drop foals that will be sold at an average
of $75 each, or come into bearing at the age of three years. It
is also assumed that the money received for half of the male
get will be used in the purchase of native mares at the prices in-

dicated, to be added to the original stud; also that the fillies born in the stud will remain to breed. Starting with 1,000 mares on this basis, the following results should be attained in the first ten years:

Years.	Breeding mares.	Males born.	No. males sold.	Average value of males.	Total value males sold.	Average price mares bought.	Number of mares bought.
1	1,000	300	150	$50.00	$7,500	$12.00	625
2	1,000	300	150	50.00	7,500	12.00	625
3	1,000	300	150	50.00	7,500	14.00	590
4	1,775	532	266	60.00	15,960	14.00	1,140
5	2,550	765	382	60.00	22,920	15.00	1,528
6	3,238	971	485	65.00	31,525	15.00	2,102
7	4,642	1,393	696	70.00	48,750	20.00	2,495
8	6,552	1,966	983	70.00	68,810	20.00	3,440
9	9,139	2,742	1,371	80.00	109,680	25.00	4,387
10	12,271	3,682	1,841	90.00	165,690	30.00	5,523
Totals	12,271	12,851	6,474	$75.04	$485,805	$21.74	22,342

In this estimate the average price of native mares has been put at $21.75, instead of $12, for which they can be bought now. This is to make allowance for any advance in price which may come from the development of this branch of the stock business. At the end of the ten years there will be on hand, if not otherwise disposed of:

1,000 superannuated mares 14 years old or older, worth say....... $ 1,500
7,384 foals, all high grades, worth say $25 each...... 184,100
5,484 yearlings, high grades, worth $50 each.................... 274,200
3,952 two-year-old grades, worth $75 each. 296,100

     Total $754,700

Sales of stallions to the people of Central America would save a part of the cost of shipping the surplus to foreign markets. Desiring to improve their stock, and having no other convenient source of supply, the people there will buy quite a number of the best young stallions in the stud at fair prices.

Mules are always in demand in the Southern States, only four days' sail from Caratasca. The larger cities of the Atlantic coast, as far north as New York will also buy large numbers of mules. In Central America mules of small size sell freely for $50 to $100 each; for exceptionally large, fine, and well-trained animals prices range as high as $150 to $300 per head. Such animals as may be gotten from the native mares by the use of large and well-bred jacks will find ready market, even for packing, at $75 to $100 and if trained properly for riding, will bring figures above the highest mentioned here. They can be raised on the Perry grant at a very small cost.

Where nature unaided produces such a profusion of food suitable for feeding swine, and where two and even three crops of corn can be grown each year, raising pigs will cost a merely nominal sum per head. In all parts of Central America pork and lard are in request at prices ranging from 12½ to 25 cents per pound. No disease of epidemic nature has been known among the hogs of Honduras, so far as has been learned.

INLAND NAVIGATION.

A system of sounds or salt water lakes, called lagoons in Spanish, extends entirely across the north line of the Perry grant, and beyond Caratasca to Cape Gracias a Dios, the easternmost point of Honduras. Nearly all of these lakes are clear, free from obstructions and deep enough for safe navigation. Very little marsh is found on their borders, the surrounding land rising at once from the water's edge to a height of from one to twelve feet, and then sloping upward. The lowest of these lands are of unsurpassed fertility and value for the growing of rice, sugarcane, breadfruit, bananas, plantains, cocoanuts, yams, cassava, sweet potatoes, arrowroot, and many other crops which thrive on moist soil. Many highly prized varieties of timber abound on these low lands, all of which are within easy reach of navigable water. Usually these sounds are separated from the sea by strips of sandy land varying from one to ten miles in width, in the middle of which there is generally a savanna from

a few rods to a few miles wide, covered by grasses. Every acre
of the coast lands can be made to yield fruits common to tropical
or   to temperate zones, such as oranges, lemons, limes, mangoes,
cashew, soursops, papayas, aguacates, rose apples, pineapples,
guavas, plums, apricots, almonds, grapes, tomatoes, coffee, cacao,
vanilla and others, while ginger, cassava, yampas, yams, arrowroot, sugarcane and cotton are grown most successfully.   But
the use for which this sandy land is best adapted, and for which
it can not be surpassed, is the growing of cocoanuts.

First in the chain of lagoons is Cape river lake which barely
touches the western line of the grant.   This lagoon is five miles
from east to west, and three miles wide.   At its western end it
receives part of the waters of the Sangrelia river, which rises
within 100 yards of the River Sico, and after flowing north
through a fertile valley, discharges part of its waters into the
sea at a point about a mile from Iriona, a port of entry on the
roadstead situated west of Cape Cameron.   On the shore of this
roadstead, which is 40 miles wide, villages are dotted at intervals
of from one to two and one-half miles.   The Sangrelia is navigable
for ten or fifteen miles, and Cape river for nearly as great a distance.

Less than two miles east of Cape River lagoon, and connected
with it by a narrow channel, is the end of La Criba lagoon,
which stretches eastward to the channel of Black river, 11 miles.
In relation to this stream and the region through which it flows,
Squier says:

Rio Tinto, Negro or Black river, which, a short distance from the sea
takes the name of Poyer, Poyas, or Polyer river, is a considerable stream,
and is said to have a course of about 120 miles. In common with most of
the rivers on the coast, it has a bad, variable bar at its mouth, on which
the water ranges, at different seasons, at from five to nine feet. Small
vessels may ascend from forty to sixty miles. It was on this river that
the English had a fort and some settlements during the last century,
which were, however, evacuated in 1786, in conformity with the treaty
that year negotiated between England and Spain. Subsequent attempts
were made to found permanent establishments there, one under the aus-
pices of the "the Cazique of Poyas," Sir Gregor McGregor, and another

in 1839-41 by an English company, under the countenance of the British settlement at Belize, but all have proved signal failures. The last adventurers named the district "Province Victoria," and made an unimportant establishment, to which they gave the name of Fort Wellington. An account of this expedition was written by Thomas Young, a person connected with it in some official capacity, which conveys considerable information concerning this portion of the coast. He describes that portion of the stream called Rio Tinto as flowing through a low, but rich and densely-wooded country, which, a few miles higher up, becomes swampy, and covered with willow trees. At the point where a branch of the main stream diverges to connect with the Criba, or Black River lagoon, commences the savanna and pine-ridge country, where some Sambos have a settlement. The savanna supports a few cattle, but the land is poor, and unfit for cultivation; "but, notwithstanding its aridity, it is very beautiful. It extends several miles in every direction, and appears to have been laid out by some landscape gardener. It is relieved by clumps of papter trees and low shrubbery, which are the haunts of many deer. There are also great quantities of lofty pine trees. Some of the pine-ridges on this coast are very extensive, and are valuable for their timber, which is the red pitch-pine, rich in turpentine. This timber, from its length and straightness, is not only very useful for building, but also for masts and spars. In the pine-ridges many mounds of earth rise above the level surface to the height of eight or ten feet, and have broad tops, large enough for dwelling-houses. Some parts of the savanna, however, are swampy, and are the nurseries of annoying insects." Above this pine-ridge the river is bordered by a continuous "bush," relieved higher up by many gracefully-bending bamboos, and the tall cabbage palm, the crown of which affords food, and the straight trunks, when split, boards for native buildings. At a point sixteen miles above the mouth of the river, the English anciently had an establishment, and here the sarsaparilla and cacao begin to make their appearance. Near this point had been anciently a coffee plantation, at a place called Lowry Hill, and near by had been a sugar estate, the boilers for which still remained at the time of Young's visit. "Thousands of banana trees, loaded with fruit, were growing spontaneously." The ground here becomes elevated, and the Poyer, or Sugar Loaf Peak, 2,000 feet high, shuts off the view seaward. Up to the "Embarcadero" the river is much obstructed by snags, which, even in small boats, it is difficult to avoid. Young adds that "the passage from Fort Wellington to the Embarcadero, during a flood in the river, takes a pitpan, with six men, three days and a half. The descent, under similar circumstances, can be made in a day and a half." The Embarcadero is estimated by Roberts (Strangeways following his authority as ninety miles from the sea, but this is probably an over-estimate.

The Poyas Indians have a number of settlements among the hills of the same name, on the upper tributaries of this river. Young reports the land about the Poyer hills as exceedingly fertile, and the country healthy.

Of Black river lagoon, which is entirely within the boundaries of this grant, he says:

Black river lagoon, called Criba by the Spaniards, according to Roberts, who visited it, is about fifteen miles long by seven wide. It contains several small islands, which were cultivated during the English occupation of Black River. At this period they erected considerable works of defense, which were enlarged by the Spaniards after the English evacuation, the ruins of which are still conspicuous. On the borders of the lagoon are some extensive savannas and pine-ridges, from which the former settlers obtained considerable quantities of pitch, tar, and turpentine.

East of Black river and connected with it and La Criba lagoon by a straight, wide and deep channel, lies Ebon lagoon, ten miles long and six wide. On the south shore of Ebon lagoon is a savanna which stretches away for miles, broken by occasional ocotals from which long-leafed pines of superior quality and size can be obtained. From the northeastern corner of Ebon lagoon extend a low place which is covered by water during the rainy seasons. Between this low place and Plantain river is a " haul-over " or portage, about a mile long. Over this the people have for generations hauled their boats. When the streams are high dories can pass from river to lagoon with little difficulty. Of Plantain river some forty or forty five miles are navigable by light draft steamers, and fifteen or twenty miles more are navigated by pipantes. A large part of this distance is through the field of wild bananas and plantains mentioned on page 24.

Between Plantain river and Brus lagoon is a low place over which canoes are paddled during the season of high water. This place is little more than a mile in width. It is believed that this, like the depression between Plantain river and Ebon lagoon, and that between the Patuca and Tilbalacca lake, was once a channel through which that stream discharged part of its current.

Brus lagoon is fifteen miles long and five to eight wide. It is comparatively shallow, and part of its bottom is covered by beds of oysters. From its shore a grassy savanna extends to the southward. Over this Consul Burchard, General Gross and others, including the government explorers whose report is quoted on page 12, traveled for days without reaching the end. The grass is good and might afford abundant grazing for thousands of stock, but the entire tract is practically unoccupied. Nearly half of the waters of the Patuca flow into Brus lagoon at its eastern end, through the broad channel, called Toomtoom, or Tcma-maya, "the white lily mouth" or entrance. Through this channel boats of large size and drawing two or three feet of water can have easy access to the Patuca, which is the largest river in the Republic, and for all purposes of navigation and lumbering is the most valuable. Squier describes the Patuca and the country along its banks as follows :

The Patook river (written Patuca by the Spaniards) enters the sea by a principal mouth about midway between Cartine (also called by the Spaniards Brus, and by the English Brewer's) and Cartago, or Carat-asca lagoons. It appears to be the largest river on the entire northern coast of Honduras, between the Ulua and Herbias, or Cape Gracias a Dios rivers. It takes its rise in the very heart of the Department of Olancho, in the vicinity of the large Spanish town of Juticalpa (capital of the department), and the great Indian town of Catacamas. The principal streams which unite to form the Patuca are the rivers Jalan, Tinto de Olancho, and the Guyape or (Guallape) and Guallambre. The two last named are celebrated for their extensive gold washings, to which reference is elsewhere made. The geographical basin in which this river collects its waters is one of the richest and most beautiful in all Central America. It is separated from the transverse valley of the Rio Herbias or Segovia by a high, narrow chain of mountains, steep on the south, but subsiding by terraces toward the north. Señor Herrera, in his report already alluded to, states that the Patuca is navigable for canoes as high as the junction of the Jalan with the Guyape. The river, however, above the coast alluvions has a powerful current and is interrupted by rapids called "chiflones." At the mouth of the Guallambre is what is called Puerto de Delon ; below this point are numerous "chiflones," the principal of which are those of Campanera and Caoba. At one point the river is compressed between high, precipitous walls of rock for a long distance. The place is called "Portal del Infierno," or Hell's Mouth, and probably gave rise to the story recorded by Roberts, "that at one part of its course the river has forced its way through a range of hills, one of which is completely excavated by the stream, which thus passes through a natural arch, as through a cavern, for a distance of nearly five hundred yards." The principal affluents below the Guallambre are the following, in the Poyas dialect, viz.: Rio Guineo, Rio Cuyamel, Rio Amis-Was (River of Bee-hives), Rio Was-Preasenla (Roaring Water), Rio Campu, and Rio Upurra (River of Retreat).

The principal mouth of the Patuca opens directly into the sea, and is obstructed by a bad, shifting bar, on which there is generally from eight to ten feet of water. Sometimes, after heavy gales, it is deeper. The tide, which is slight, nevertheless ebbs and flows in the river for some miles. The land about the mouth of the river is mostly savanna, which, however, according to an account given in 1844 by Messrs. Haly, Upton, and Deacon, unlike most of the savannas on the coast, is not swampy, and furthermore has a black and fertile soil. An extensive pine-ridge is found about thirty miles up the river, above which, as also down to near the sea, the banks are thickly wooded, having a great variety of soil—red clay, loam, and black mold—all admirably adapted to the cultivation of sugar, coffee, cotton, cacao, indigo, etc. Large quantities of mahogany, cedar, rose, and santa maria wood are found throughout the whole length of the river valley, while the pine-ridges are capable of furnishing inexhaustible quantities of pine wood and oak. Exclusive of valuable woods, the forests produce abundance of sarsaparilla, India rubber, gum copal, and vanilla. Mr. Haly pronounces the Patuca "navigable for small steamers" to the vicinity of the Spanish settlements in Olancho, "or at least to the foot of the falls" (Portal del Infierno), and that "it is the best river on the entire coast, excepting that of San Juan de Nicaragua, for commercial intercourse with the interior." He thinks also, that an establishment at its mouth, supported by improvements in the river and by roads in the interior, would soon become the most important point on the coast east of Omoa. Roberts estimates the length of the Patuca at one hundred and fifty miles, and Strangeways at one hundred miles. Various establishments of Caribs and Sambos exist on the lower part of the river, and the Toncas and Poyas (called Payas by the Spaniards) on its upper waters and its various tributaries.

An arm of the Patuca, called Toomtoom creek, diverging from the main stream in a short distance above its mouth, connects it with Brus, or Brewer's lagoon. This lagoon has a wide mouth, but will not admit vessels drawing more than six or seven feet. Three or four miles from its entrance is an island of moderate height, about two miles in circumference, fertile, formerly fortified by the English, and seems to have been extensively cultivated. This lagoon abounds with fine fish, has plenty of water-fowl, and large beds of oysters. "The country to the northward," says Roberts, "is beautifully diversified by gently-rising hills, valleys, and savannas, and the soil, generally speaking is excellent."

The Patuca offers the only direct and easy route for transportation between the sea and the richest mines and most extensive system of valleys in Honduras. Below the mouth of the Guampu the river is now navigable for steamers of light draft, the only obstacles being a few rocks at one place, some snags which can be readily removed, and three or four sand bars which had twelve to sixteen inches of water at the end of the last dry season. These can be quickly dug out or deepened when required, by means with which every man familiar with the management of stern wheel steamers is acquainted. These bars will obstruct navigation only during the lowest stage of water. Three or four hours work and a few dynamite cartridges will suffice for the removal of all the rocks in the way. Not far above the Guampu the current of the Patuca is broken by the Caoba rapids, and beyond those it is interrupted by falls at the Campanero, at Puerto del Infierno and at Puerto de Delon, the last two practically impassable.

About twenty-four miles south from the coast the Patuca approaches within five miles of Tilbalacca lagoon, which connects by a wide channel with Gauranta lagoon, and this in its turn with Caratasca lake. From the southwestern corner of Tilbalacca a bayou extends toward the Patuca, and from the latter what seems to have once been the bed of the river reaches out toward the bayou. It is generally believed by those acquainted with the locality that the Patuca once flowed into Tilbalacca. It is currently reported that when the river is high the natives paddle their canoes across this place from river to lagoon.

Tibacunta Creek enters the sea about thirty-two miles to the westward of the entrance of Caratasca. It may serve to carry away some of the high water in the rainy season but in ordinary stages of water it will do little if any more than furnish a convenient way by which tracts of fruit land s may be reached by boats.

Squier said of Caratasca, some forty years ago, what is essentially true to-day, that:

Carataska or Cartago lagoon "is of very considerable extent, varying in breadth, and having, in some places, the appearance of several lagoons running into each other, in various directions, for the most part parallel to the coast, but nowhere exceeding twelve miles in breadth." It has two entrances, one a small creek called "Tibacunta." The principal mouth is wide, with thirteen or fourteen feet of water on the bar. The lagoon is estimated at about thirty-six miles in length. It is for the most part shallow, varying in depth, from six to twelve and eighteen feet. Captain Henderson, who visited it in 1804, describes the country near the Sambo village of Crata (Cronch or Cartago) as " a spacious savanna of very considerable extent, forming an entire level of unbroken verdure and finest pasturage, skirted on one side by the waters of the lagoon, and on the other bounded by gently rising hills. The clumps of pine and other lofty trees, interpersed at pleasing distances over the whole gave the view all the appearance of cultivated art, and afforded a most agreeable relief to the eye." Several small streams discharge into the lagoon from the south, viz.: Ibentara, Cartago, Locca, Warunta and Kaukari. It has also three considerable islands. There are a number of villages of Sambos around this lagoon, who raise a few cattle, but do not cultivate the soil to any extent, being grossly indolent and improvident. "The land in the vicinity of the lagoon," according to Roberts, " consists almost entirely of extensive and beautiful savannas, covered with the finest pasturage, and abounding in deer and other game. There are a few pine trees at Crata, but on the opposite or south side there are ridges growing timber as large as any on the coast. Behind these ridges the savannas are bounded by hills, whose summits are covered by the most luxuriant vegetation. On the banks of the streams in the interior there is excellent mahogany, and cedar of the finest quality and largest size. Pimento and various other valuable plants are also indigenous."

Caratasca, half inclosed by the grant, is as perfectly land-locked, quiet and commodious a harbor as can be needed for all the vessels that can ever be required for fully serving the commerce of the country naturally tributary to the Patuca valley. It is separated from the sea by long spits which are usually sandy; but at a point about five miles west of the entrance there is an area of clay which rises from six to ten feet above tide. This offers an excellent site for warehouses and other buildings required for transportation business. On the shoalest place in the channel connecting the lake with the ocean there are fifteen feet of water at low tide. A few hundred feet from the beach, and a little to the westward of the center line of the channel, is a small key which perfectly protects the entrance to the channel from the waves caused by northerly winds. For one hundred miles off the entrance the water is only ten to thirty fathoms deep. Vessels can not only enter there for cargo at any time, but they can find protection there from heavy gales. Any craft finding difficulty or danger in entering, or any driven to leeward of the entrance in a northerly gale, could find a perfectly safe lee and good anchorage in five to ten fathoms under Cape Gracias, only forty miles to the southeast. These and other facts warrant the claim that Caratasca is the best harbor on the whole north and east coast of Central America. It forms a beginning for the system of inland navigation which gives command of every part of this grant, and offers gateways over which heavy machinery, tools and other things required in the gold and silver bearing districts of the Republic may be carried safely, quickly and cheaply, and the fine woods and other products of the country brought out.

To make this natural system of inland navigation most useful the lagoons and rivers must be connected by cutting canals through the few and narrow places where they are now separated. Two miles of canal will connect Sangrelia river, Cape river and lagoon, Black river and Ebon lagoon. Four miles more of canal will connect Ebon lagoon, Plantain river, Brus lagoon Tomamaya river and the Patuca. It is asserted by those who have long been acquainted with this locality that a few hundred yards of cutting will suffice to open a good channel from the Patuca to Tilbalacca lagoon. Assuming that it will be necessary to dig three miles of canal there, it follows that, by making nine or ten miles of canal through low land, entirely free from rock and largely in sand and alluvial deposits, between 250 and 350 miles of perfectly safe river lagoon and navigation will be connected with Caratasca harbor and the sea. This will give to fruit growers and others who may settle on any of the hundreds of square miles of rich land around these lakes or along the banks of these rivers, easy and cheap transportation to market, and frequent communication with the outside world. Such canals will undoubtedly be made within the next three years, perhaps within the next twelvemonth, by the American Honduras Company.

A good wagon road from the head of navigation of the Patuca to the valley of Juticalpa, and along that valley to the capital of the Department of Olancho would do more than all other causes combined have done for the development of central and eastern Honduras. For carrying goods from this city to the coast the charge is 7½ cents per pound, or $150 per ton; nor can the muleteers do the work for less without losing money. The consequence is that the valleys and hillsides where sugar, coffee, rice, and other products wanted in foreign markets might be grown with a minimum outlay, are neglected. The cost of transortation to market leaves nothing for the producer, and he is wise enough to do nothing for nothing rather than work for nothing. At Juticalpa the Guayape, the Jalan, and the Lepaguara meet to form the Patuca, which the Guayambre joins a few miles away. Each of these rivers rises in a rich gold or silver-producing region, where mines can not now be profitably opened nor worked, because the difficulty—practically the impossibility— of introducing such machinery as is necessary to successful mining prevents. All of these rivers flow through valleys the soil of which is rich, yielding most abundantly when tilled; but not a thousandth part is cultivated.

Near the city of Juticalpa the river Telica enters the Patuca, after draining the valley of Manto, famed for its excellent mules and horses, its productive cane fields and coffee plantations, and its gold, silver and copper deposits. Near the valley of Manto is the beautiful valley of Agalta, forty miles long, and from ten to twenty miles wide, rich in stock and capable of supporting thousands of inhabitants more than it has. It is of these mountain valleys that Consul Burchard wrote: "Here the northern man can, by a minimum of labor, provide for himself the comforts and luxuries of both tropical and temperate zones." Here is that land which may well be destined to become the home of that high degree of civilization which " is possible only where the possession of plants that yield abundant food for a moderate outlay of labor, allows, with due toil and foresight, a large degree of leisure and relief from intent anxiety."

The opening and maintenance of a route from the interior to the ocean will make possible the full development of this cool and healthful country. New mines will be opened and old ones will be worked more extensively than ever before. Food will be needed for their laborers, and intelligent agriculture will be stimulated to supply the home demand. The opening of a route over which the products of farms can be cheaply carried to market will further encourage farming. All this will give employment and good wages to thousands who now earn but a scant subsistance in a country where a living need cost but a fraction of the sum required to support a person in the northern States. New enterprises of various kinds will be called into activity and old ones will be so quickened into new life that Juticalpa will resume the position she long held as the commercial center of all these mineral districts and fertile valleys. All the surplus products of the surrounding forests, mines and farms will flow to Juticalpa, for transportation to the markets of the outer world, and in return will be brought comforts and luxuries now beyond the reach of the people.

LABORERS.

In reply to queries relating to the number and character of laborers to be found in the region of this grant, an ex-governor of Mosquitia whose statements have before been quoted in these pages, says:

The Province of Mosquitia (now called Colon) contains four kinds of laborers. First, the Caribs, who are without doubt the most hardy, industrious, and reliable. In strength and endurance they will compare favorably with the southern negro or the northern lumberman. They all speak English, and constitute a very important element in the mahogany works and sugar plantations of British Honduras.

The Sambo or Mosquito Indian ranks next to the Carib, and is in some respects preferable to him as a laborer. His strength and powers of endurance are less, but he is more obedient and respectful. He looks on his employer as his master, and gives him the homage and obedience of a slave. The women and children are accustomed to outdoor labor, and are always willing to work for beads, trinkets, bright-colored calicoes, etc.

Toward the head waters of the Plantain river, and between the rivers Paulaya and Sico, we find the remnants of an Indian tribe called Poyas, which would also furnish a good number of men and women as laborers. I have frequently employed them, and found them always extremely docile, obedient, and industrious. They are very timid, and would have to be worked in gangs by themselves. For clearing and harvesting the banana fields of Plantain river they would be invaluable.

The last and most numerous in the list of laborers is the common mozo or peon of the interior, who is the most intelligent of them all. He will work well for two, three or perhaps six months, and will do all in his power to gain the confidence and esteem of his employer. His aim and intention are to get in debt as deeply as possible, and then run away. I am happy to say that there are many worthy exceptions to this rule.

Tramps and idlers can, by the laws of Honduras, be compelled to work when their labor is required or solicited, either by individuals or corporations. By judicious management the company will have no difficulty in obtaining a sufficient number of laborers, at prices ranging from $5 to $12 a month.

PRICES OF LAND.

By a decree published last March, the government of Honduras fixed the following prices for national lands: For grazing, or broken mountain lands covered by grass, $20 per caballeria; for farming or arable lands, suitable for growing grain, $30 per caballeria; for lands on the banks of navigable rivers, lakes, inland channels or the sea, or near railway lines, not less than $100 per caballeria. In one of his recent reports to the Department of State the American consul at Tegucigalpa says that a caballeria is equal to 33½ acres,

THE GOVERNMENT AND ITS POLICY.

The government of Honduras is republican in form, its constitution guaranteeing to

Every native or naturalized Honduranean freedom to profess both privately and publicly the religion he desires. The Government acknowledges no State religion. There is no censorship over the press. Everyone can follow the profession or industry he chooses, and may go from one republic to the other without passports. One may dispose of his property as he sees fit. The constitution grants no privileges of caste. Before the law all are equal. All citizens, except criminals, may fill public posts. Both natives and foreigners are equal before the civil law.

One year's residence in Honduras entitles foreigners to naturalization, to-wit: Colonists who occupy lands in Indian neighborhoods, or in unsettled districts; all who inaugurate important works of general utility; those who bring fortunes into the country; all who introduce useful inventions into the Republic, and all who procure naturalization papers from the proper authorities.

All Honduraneans, both natives and naturalized foreigners, who have professions, income, means of support or property; and all natives or naturalized foreigners of the age of 18 who are married, and who can read and write are citizens at the age of 21.

The constitution guarantees all Honduraneans individual equality and security of life and property.

The constitution guarantees the right of *habeas corpus*. The privilege of self-defense is inviolable. Torture is abolished forever. Precautions and restrictions that are not absolutely necessary for the security of prisoners are prohibited.

The domestic hearth, correspondence (epistolary), telegraphic messages, private papers and books used in commerce are inviolable.

No inhabitant shall be molested for the expression of his opinions, no matter of what nature they may be, if such opinions infringe no law; nor for any act that does not disturb the public peace.

Police regulations are exercised solely by the civil authorities.

No one may be deprived of his property except by course of law or by sentence of law. Condemnation for public benefit must be certified by law, or by sentence founded in law: but in no case without indemnification. Confiscation is abolished forever.

Each author or inventor has the sole right to his work or invention.

No foreigner shall be entitled to more privileges than any other; but all possess the same civil rights as native Honduraneans. Foreigners may, in consequence, buy, sell, locate, exercise arts and professions, possess all kinds of property and dispose of it in the form prescribed by law; enter the country and leave it with their property, and frequent with their ships the ports and navigate the rivers of the Republic. They are exempt from extraordinary contributions and are guaranteed entire liberty in commerce, and may construct temples and churches or establish cemeteries in any part of the Republic. Their marriage contracts shall not be invalidated, if not in conformity with certain religious beliefs, if they have been legally celebrated. They are not obliged to become naturalized. They may vote for public offices, according to law, which in no case excludes them on account of their origin.

The President is General Luis Bogran, lineal descendant of an ancient noble Norman family. For many years he has been recognized as leader in the work of promoting the material, social and political welfare of his country. To this end he has labored constantly and earnestly for the development of the agriculture of Honduras, showing firm belief in the principle announced by *La Republica*, the ministerial newspaper, when, speaking of the Perry grant, it said: "Development of its agricultural and mineral resources is the safest, surest and most permanently beneficial of all means for increasing the prosperity, wealth, and power of a nation. Recognizing this truth it is the policy of the government of Honduras to encourage by every means in its power the peaceful cultivation of the fertile soil of this Republic. The government has repeatedly declared that it ' takes the agricultural industry under its especial care.' "

Of all the many mining and other grants made by Honduras not one has been ignored, violated or set aside by the government; but, on the other hand, the government has repeatedly extended the time allowed for performance by the grantees of acts agreed on, and has renewed contracts which had become void through failure of the contractors to do their work. Americans have been especially favored ever since the negotiations between the United States and Great Britain, in 1852, resulted in the relinquishment by England of all claim to territory belonging to Honduras.

Under the administration of President Bogran the public debt is being reduced, public schools are being established and their usefulness increased, industrial arts are encouraged and disaffection and disturbance of the public peace quietly avoided. In every part of the land, and in every class of society, the careful observer finds one uniform sentiment of contentment with existing conditions and the promise of improvement they give. The lower orders are never in favor of any disturbance through which the men may be dragged into military service. The higher orders are all engaged directly or indirectly in business, usually in trade, and are wise enough to see that disastrous loss to themselves is sure to result from anything which seriously deranges public affairs, therefore the influence of the leading classes is firmly against all disorder. Many years have passed since this Republic was the scene of even an attempt at rebellion, and the fate of all filibustering schemes of recent years shows conclusively that the people, as individuals, are as determined as the government is to promptly put down all such attempts to disturb the peace. This feeling will increase in strength as the masses realize more clearly than they do now, that nothing but evil results from unlawful acts directed against the legitimate government.

PUBLIC OPINION.

As tending to show the popular feeling in Honduras toward the enterprise of the American-Honduras Company; the subjoined articles are quoted from the newspapers published in Tegucigalpa, the national capital of the Republic. The first is from *La Nacion* of March 23, 1888:

Two years ago capitalists in the United States were considering the project of establishing the business of canning beef in Honduras. Wanting full, acurate and trustworthy information about the Republic, its cattle and its capacity for producing beeves, these capitalists induced an agent of the United States Department of Agriculture to make an examination of Honduras and its resources. That gentleman, for years widely known as an expert in affairs relating to live-stock interests, made a thorough study of the agricultural resources of this country. His report was very favorable, and the capitalists determined to engage in the business of canning beef here; but since that report was made prices of cattle have been so very low in the United States that beef could be canned there almost as cheaply as it could be canned here. Yet a factory would have been put into operation here, despite that unfavorable circumstance, if strikes among the laborers in Chicago had not discouraged new enterprises.

The agent referred to above, Mr. E. W. Perry, of Chicago, was very strongly impressed in favor of Honduras, his years of study of the agriculture of different countries enabling him to estimate at their true value the opportunities offered by the untilled valleys and hills of Honduras. The consequence was that he applied, last year, to this Government for a concession of a large tract of land in a little-known portion of the Department of Colon. Every detail of this application was most carefully studied in regard to its bearing on the interests and welfare of the people of the Republic, as well as in its legal aspects. The suggestions of the Governor of the Department of Colon and of the Attorney-General of the Republic were duly considered; conditions requiring the performance of public works of incalculable benefit to the people were rigidly insisted upon, and stipulations fully protecting and guaranteeing all legally acquired rights of the Indians and others residing on those lands, were agreed upon before the Government issued its decree ratifying the contract.

The region covered by this decree is a part of an almost uninhabited wilderness. Only a few wild Indians have homes there, and to them the decree secures all their legal rights. In carrying out the contract with the government Mr. Perry, and those who may be associated with him, will need the labor of these Indians, and of many other people, and in payment for this labor must bring to and distribute in this country a large amount of capital.

The lands covered by this contract have never brought any revenue to help pay the necessary expenses of this Republic. They have, on the contrary, been a cause of annoyance, controversy and very grave international complications. Until 1850 they were claimed by Great Britain, and in later years by the neighboring friendly Republic of Nicaragua. Under the conditions of this contract with Mr. Perry this vast region must quickly begin to help the people of all Honduras. The contract demands that a large cattle estate shall be established on the lands: this will necessarily make a home market for Honduras cattle. It is required that a great wagon road shall be made and maintained, a telegraph line constructed, sawmills erected and other things done, all without cost to the government or the people of this Republic.

Thus it is apparent that this is the most important concession or contract made by this government, for the purpose of promoting the development of the agricultural resources with which every part of Honduras is so richly endowed by nature. It must bring into and distribute in this country an immense and ever-increasing amount of capital, for it is very evident that it is impossible for the contractor to gain anything through this agreement without first inducing people to cultivate that wilderness—for it can not be put aboard a ship and carried away. The land and all estates and enterprises established on it must remain a part of the Republic.

The second article is from *Honduras Progress*, a weekly paper printed in English in Tegucigalpa, and edited by a gentleman who has for years held the position of government geologist.   He says:

The government has just concluded a contract with Mr. E. W. Perry, of Chicago, under which he gets a tract of lands in the department of Colon, on condition that he shall open up in that department lumber, stock-growing and agricultural enterprises on a large scale. This is a wise step in that direction, as it will make that hitherto unprofitable section one of the richest farming regions in this or any other country. It is a section susceptible of the very highest culture. Bananas, plantains and other fruits grow spontaneously, showing that they only need a little care of man to turn them into rich sources of wealth. Apart from this, the land is abundantly watered with healthful streams, and covered the year round with native, succulent grasses, making it a very paradise for cattle and horses, and with no freezes or storms of winter to disturb them. Besides much of the land is fertile and capable of producing the maximum amount of all kinds of agricultural products. Bordering on the ocean, there is no necessity for a railroad, which circumstance undoubtedly gives it a further advantage, as railroads too often take to themselves the best profits of enterprises, leaving the producers only just enough to encourage them to work on. But this needs no railroads to connect it with the highest markets of the world. The broad Atlantic touches it and invites to its shores the competing demands of the whole of Europe and America.

These advantages assure the early and complete success of this new enterprise; and this success means much for Honduras. It will convince the world that there are other resources than mines here, most richly deserving the cultivation of outsiders. It will draw to us the attention of a substantial class of capitalists. It will bring about a diversity of industries, pursuits, and interests, without which this country can never prosper as it should. And in this respect it will be worth far more to Honduras than any price that could have been paid for the land. It is a building up of waste places—a planting of a garden in a wilderness, not to be shipped away to enrich other lands, but to remain forever as a part and parcel of Honduras.

Agriculture is the basis and supporter of all other pursuits. It is well known that the building up of the agricultural wealth of a country insures its most lasting good. California was a howling, dreary wilderness, but the gold-hunters of '49 discovered to the world its varied resources, and now we see it not broken and torn all over by the relentless tools of the miner, but dressed and smiling with richest fruits and sweet-scented fields—a veritable garden upon the face of the earth. So mote it be with Honduras, and God speed the day.

In its issue of April 7, *La Republica,* the ministerial paper, thus outlined the policy of the national Government in relation to the development of agriculture, and especially in regard to the Perry grant:

Development of its agricultural and mineral resources is the safest, surest and most permanently beneficial of all means for increasing the prosperity, wealth and power of a nation. Recognizing this truth, it is the established policy of the government of Honduras to encourage by every means in its power the peaceful cultivation of the fertile soil of this Republic. The government has repeatedly declared that it "takes the agricultural industry under its especial care."

To be able to successfully compete with farmers of other and even less favored lands, it is necessary that the people of this country should adopt, to some extent at least, the methods now so profitably followed in agriculture in those other lands. The rigors of a climate where cattle by thousands and people by hundreds perish of cold in winter, and heat far more intense than is ever felt in Honduras, parches the fields in summer, have compelled people there to invent many devices for getting a large return for their labor. They have invented machinery that can do quickly and well all the work now done by hand here. They have developed trees, plants and fruits much superior to those of the same species grown in Honduras, and have created improved breeds of cattle, horses, swine and other domesticated animals of superior size, quality, and value. The result is that the United States, our neighbor and friend of the North, has become a nation so rich that it has now in its treasury hundreds of millions of dollars for which it has no use; it has become so powerful that all other nations of earth respect its wishes and are careful to not encroach upon its rights.

It is through the adoption of improved systems of agriculture that Brazil and others of the Spanish American countries, which occupy by far the larger and naturally richer part of the New World, are so rapidly growing in wealth and power. It will be by the use of such means that Honduras—blessed above all others in the evenness and mildness of its temperature, in its healthfulness, in abundance and purity of water supply, in fertility of soil, and in geographical location—will yet take a place among the most solidly prosperous of the Republics of the Western hemisphere.

Desiring earnestly to hasten the coming of this change, which will bring an era of plenty and peaceful content, the government repeatedly urged upon the attention of the people of Honduras, and has offered to those of other countries who are skilled in agriculture and other useful arts, liberal inducements to make their homes on and cultivate lands not otherwise occupied. Citizens of other countries have been guaranteed the unmolested exercise of nearly all rights and privileges enjoyed by the citizens of Honduras. Not a single instance has been known in which the life, liberty and property of law abiding foreigners have not been properly respected and protected by this government.

In pursurance of its announced policy for fostering the agricultural interests of the country, and following the example of other administrations here, and of other countries as well, this administration has granted some concessions for that purpose. Of all that have been granted none have been of greater importance, none have been more carefully calculated to secure great and lasting benefit to the people of all classes in Honduras, than the contract made last week with Mr. E. W. Perry, of Chicago. By this contract he is required to cultivate and otherwise improve a large tract of land in Musquitia. This whole region has never produced revenue for the people of this Republic. It is, in fact, almost entirely unpopulated, except by a few scattered families of Indians. The rights of all these people are protected in the contract intended to bring about the development of this region, which has been for centuries an untamed wilderness, but may by the exercise of skill, energy and unlimited capital, be made the home of thousands of prosperous and happy Honduranians.

The full development of this enterprise will require the investment of a vast amount of money, the employment of multitudes of laborers and the importation of many improved animals, machines, and methods. All of these will become permanently a part of Honduras. All people who may make their homes on those lands become people of Honduras; every estate, every factory, mill or shop established there, become part of Honduras: in fact the whole grand undertaking is an Honduras enterprise, a part of this Republic forever.

VALUABLE WOODS AND MEDICINAL PLANTS.

Below is a very incomplete list of the valuable woods and medicinal plants found on the lands of The American-Honduras Company.

Mahogany, rosewood, lignum vitæ, mulberry, sandalwood, copaiva, liquid amber, copal, India-rubber, pine, cedar, silk, cotton tree, live oak, cypress, rourou, tuno, santa marie, mangrove, ironwood, calabash, algarroba, breadfruit, orange, lemon, lime, myrtle, laurel, ebony—both black and white, quince, walnut, locust, allspice, tamarind, cassia fistula, chicory, artemesia silvestris, indigo, white locust, tobacco, capsicum, Solanum grandiflora, S. nigrum, S. esculentum, S. mammosum, S. tuberosum, and scores of others known in the arts or in medicine.

Of the fine woods many are unknown in the markets of the United States, where they will sell freely and at very high prices as soon as a judicious effort shall have been made to show their beauty and utility.

www.ingramcontent.com/pod-product-compliance
Lightning Source LLC
Chambersburg PA
CBHW022034080426
42733CB00007B/829